Your Favorite Authors

Jerry Pinkney

by Lisa M. Bolt Simons

CAPSTONE PRESS
a capstone imprint

First Facts are published by Capstone Press,
1710 Roe Crest Drive, North Mankato, Minnesota 56003
www.mycapstone.com

Library of Congress Cataloging-in-Publication Data
Names: Simons, Lisa M. B., 1969– author.
Title: Jerry Pinkney / by Lisa M. Bolt Simons.
Description: North Mankato, Minnesota : Capstone Press, 2017. | Series: First facts.
Your favorite authors | Includes bibliographical references and index.
Identifiers: LCCN 2016023238| ISBN 9781515735571 (library binding) |
ISBN 9781515735625 (pbk.) | ISBN 9781515735663 (ebook pdf)
Subjects: LCSH: Pinkney, Jerry—Juvenile literature. | Illustrators—United States—Biography—
Juvenile literature. | African American illustrators—Biography—Juvenile literature.
Classification: LCC NC975.5.P56 S56 2017 | DDC 741.6092 [B]—dc23
LC record available at https://lccn.loc.gov/2016023238

Editorial Credits
Carrie Braulick Sheely and Michelle Hasselius, editors; Kayla Dohmen, designer;
Ruth Smith, media researcher; Gene Bentdahl, production specialist

Photo Credits
Alamy Images: B Christopher, 19 bottom; Associated Press: Dake Kang, 15, 17; Capstone
Press: Michael Byers, cover; Getty Images: Richard Cummins, 11; Newscom: Jeff Malet
Photography, 13, 19 top, RON TARVER/MCT, 21; Shutterstock: donfiore, cover, background
design elements, f11photo, 7, Julia Snegireva, cover, background design elements, Namning,
5 top, pixelheadphoto, 9, Zerbor, 5 bottom

Printed in the United States of America.
092016   010030S17

Table of Contents

Chapter 1: Artist As a Living

Jerry Pinkney worked at a newsstand when he was 12. He sold newspapers to John Liney every day. Liney was a famous cartoonist. One day Liney saw Pinkney sketching. He asked to see Pinkney's sketchbook. Liney invited Pinkney to his studio. He encouraged Pinkney to continue sketching. Pinkney realized he could make a living doing something he loved. He grew up to become an award-winning illustrator.

Chapter 2: Encouragement and Honors

Jerry Pinkney was born in Philadelphia, Pennsylvania, on December 22, 1939. He had five brothers and sisters. His family lived in a neighborhood with people from many **cultures**. The Pinkneys didn't have a TV. They had one radio. Pinkney's parents encouraged their children to draw and be creative.

---

culture—a group of people's beliefs, customs, and way of life

Philadelphia, Pennsylvania

"What I try to do with my art is speak about my feelings or express my feelings about the world we live in. We live in a country that, happily, is very diverse."—Jerry Pinkney

diverse—unlike others; different

Pinkney has **dyslexia**. But he didn't know until he was an adult. Pinkney struggled with reading and spelling. But his mom encouraged him to find something he liked to do. Pinkney was talented at drawing. This talent made up for his challenges. Pinkney worked hard in school. He graduated from elementary school with **honors**.

---

dyslexia—a learning disability that is usually marked by problems in reading, spelling, and writing

honors—recognition given to high-achieving students when they graduate

Hard Work Recognized

In 2003 Pinkney received an award from The Lab School in Washington, D.C. The school is for children with learning disabilities. People who receive this award have done outstanding work in their careers, despite having learning disabilities.

Pinkney's family continued to encourage him. His dad always tried to find art classes for his son to take. In high school Pinkney studied **commercial** art. Then he attended the Philadelphia Museum School of Art on a **scholarship**. Pinkney's first illustration job was creating greeting cards.

---

commercial—creative work used mostly for advertising

scholarship—money given to a student to help pay for school

"When I'm working on a book, I wish the phone would never ring. I love doing it. My satisfaction comes from the actual marks on the paper … it's magic."—Jerry Pinkney

The Philadelphia Museum School of Art is now called the University of the Arts.

Chapter 3: "Storyteller at Heart"

Pinkney's first illustrated book was *The Adventures of Spider: West African Folk Tales.* It came out in 1964. The same year Pinkney received an award from the Boston Art Directors' Club. In 1981 Pinkney won his first Coretta Scott King Honor Award for *Count On Your Fingers African Style.*

Pinkney signs books at the 10th annual National Book Festival
in Washington, D.C.

Pinkney creates artwork for stories that remind him of his childhood. He wants his projects to celebrate **multiculturalism** and Black America. His book about African-American folk hero John Henry is one example. The book won a Caldecott Honor in 1995.

---

multiculturalism—involving people from different races or religions

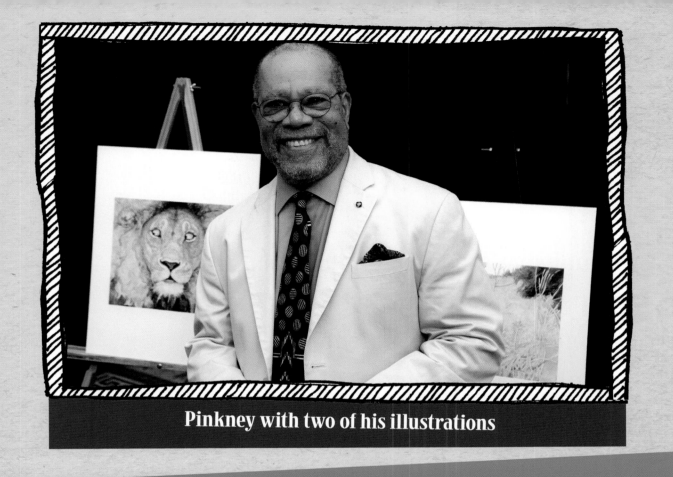

Pinkney with two of his illustrations

Award Winner

Pinkney has received more than 100 awards for his work. Six of his books have received Caldecott awards. The Caldecotts go to the best picture books each year.

Pinkney uses watercolor in his work. But he has his own technique and style. Pinkney is not afraid to try new things. He used **collage** in a book for the first time in 2009. That same year he published *The Lion and the Mouse*. It was his first wordless book. The book won the Caldecott Medal in 2010. Pinkney continues to illustrate award-winning books.

---

collage—a type of art that is made by attaching different materials to a flat surface or by using different styles in an illustration

Pinkney signs copies of his book, *The Lion and the Mouse*.

"I'm a storyteller at heart."
—Jerry Pinkney

Pinkney does more than illustrate books. He teaches art in colleges. He created art for *National Geographic* magazine and the National Parks Service. He designed postage stamps. Pinkney's work has been on TV. Some of his art is displayed around the world.

A fan holds up one of Pinkney's books

Pinkney designed a postage stamp of Jackie Robinson.

Chapter 4: Lifetime Artist

Pinkney won two lifetime achievement awards in 2016. One was the Laura Ingalls Wilder Award. He also won the Coretta Scott King-Virginia Hamilton Award for Lifetime Achievement. As a child Pinkney was encouraged to be creative. This encouragement helped him achieve many things.

Pinkney looks at drafts for *Sweethearts of Rhythm*.

"So certainly you have to put ages on a book so they know where to place it, but really, literature at its best really touches on us all. It brings us all in."—Jerry Pinkney

Timeline

1939 born in Philadelphia

1957 starts school at Philadelphia Museum School of Art

1964 starts illustrating children's books; publishes
The Adventures of Spider: West African Folk Tales

1981 wins first Coretta Scott King Honor for
Count On Your Fingers African Style

1989 wins first Caldecott Honor for *Mirandy and Brother Wind*;
book also wins the Coretta Scott King Award

1990 wins his second Caldecott Honor for *The Talking Eggs*

1995 wins his third Caldecott Honor for *John Henry*

1997 wins Coretta Scott King Award for *Minty: A Story of Young
Harriet Tubman*

2000 wins Caldecott Honor for *The Ugly Duckling*

2002 wins Coretta Scott King Award for *Goin' Someplace Special*

2003 wins Caldecott Honor for *Noah's Ark*

2009 wins Coretta Scott King Honor for *The Moon Over Star*

2010 wins the Caldecott Medal for *The Lion and the Mouse*

2016 wins Laura Ingalls Wilder Award and Coretta Scott
King-Virginia Hamilton Award for Lifetime Achievement

Glossary

collage (kuh-LAHZH)—a type of art that is made by attaching different materials to a flat surface or by using different styles in an illustration

commercial (kuh-MUHR-shuhl)—creative work used mostly for advertising

culture (KUHL-chuhr)—a group of people's beliefs, customs, and way of life

diverse (dih-VERSS)—unlike others; different

dyslexia (dis-LEK-see-uh)—a learning disability that is usually marked by problems in reading, spelling, and writing

honors (ON-urz)—recognition given to high-achieving students when they graduate

multiculturalism (muhl-ti-KUHL-chuh-ruhl-iz-uhm)—involving people from different races or religions

scholarship (SKOL-ur-ship)—money given to a student to help pay for school

Read More

Bolte, Mari. *Drawing Faces: A Step-by-Step Sketchbook.* My First Sketchbook. North Mankato, Minn.: Capstone Press, 2015.

Llanas, Sheila Griffin. *Jerry Pinkney.* Children's Illustrators. Minneapolis: ABDO Pub. Co., 2012.

Internet Sites

FactHound offers a safe, fun way to find Internet sites related to this book. All of the sites on FactHound have been researched by our staff.

Here's all you do:

Visit *www.facthound.com*

Type in this code: 9781515735571

Index

Check out projects, games and lots more at **www.capstonekids.com**